FOSTER CHILDREN

RUTH ABRAMS

WestBow Press books may be ordered through booksellers or by contacting:

WestBow Press
A Division of Thomas Nelson & Zondervan
1663 Liberty Drive
Bloomington, IN 47403
www.westbowpress.com
844-714-3454

Scripture taken from the New King James Version®. Copyright © 1982 by Thomas Nelson. Used by permission. All rights reserved.

ISBN: 978-1-6642-7939-1 (sc)
ISBN: 978-1-6642-7938-4 (e)

Library of Congress Control Number: 2022917977

Print information available on the last page.

WestBow Press rev. date: 11/17/2022

WestBow
PRESS®
A DIVISION OF THOMAS NELSON
& ZONDERVAN

Foster Children was written and
illustrated by Ruth Abrams.

There are many different types of families, but every single family is unique. We all have moments when we just want to give up because we don't understand why we are going through so many hardships in our lives. Sometimes it even feels like we are the only family who is struggling, but the reality is that we are not the only family who has problems. Many even think, If I belonged to a different family, things could be different. But what if I told you your family can be different without you changing families? Let me tell you a story.

There was once a lady named Grace. She loved helping people. She was kind, gentle, caring, funny, friendly, and very loving toward others. One day while she was having dinner with her family, she got a phone call. It was her friend Lucia.

"Hello, Grace," Lucia said, sounding nervous and very worried.

Grace asked, "Lucia, what happened? Are you OK?"

Lucia explained that her sister-in-law Susana had had difficulties with her family and now it was something very serious.

Grace couldn't believe it. She asked Lucia, "What can I do to help?"

Lucia said, "Well, my husband and I are on our way to their house."

Grace, not hesitating, said to Lucia, "I'll be there right away."

Grace then explained to her husband and her children what had happened, got into her car, and left.

Once she arrived at the house, there was Lucia with her husband. Grace got out of the car, went inside the house with them, and to their surprise, there was a huge mess because the police were looking for something. But Grace didn't know what it was.

Then Grace suggested to Lucia and her husband to go to the police station and see what was going on, so they all drove there. After they arrived, they saw Susana's four children, but they couldn't talk to them. They just waved at them from a glass door. Susana and her husband were nowhere to be found.

While they were waiting, a lady came out with a lot of papers in her hands and asked, "Is there anyone here for Susana?" Lucia, her husband, and Grace stood up right away and said, "Yes, we are here."

She then said, "My name is Julie. I am a social worker who is going to be handling this case.
Are you family?"

Lucia responded, "Yes, she's my sister-in-law."

And Grace said, "I'm just a very close friend
of the family."

The social worker said, "The children will need a
place to stay while this situation is solved."

Grace called her husband and told him the situation,
and her husband agreed for Grace to help the
children in any possible way. Then they both offered
their houses, but in the end, the social worker picked
the house she thought was the best option for the
children. She picked Grace's house.

Early the next morning, before she began preparing everything for her friends' children, she woke her children and explained everything that was about to happen. Her children agreed to help and even gave up their bedrooms. Since they were arriving that day, she emptied one of her children's rooms. She put on clean linen and prepared a huge meal for everyone. Finally, the social worker arrived to drop off the children. Grace and her family welcomed everyone.

The next day, Grace sat at the table with the two older new children and asked about their regular schedule when they lived with their mom and dad. She had a paper and pen ready and wrote everything down. She then began to plan whom she was going to drop off and pick up first from school. She organized herself very well. She also went to the children's schools to leave her personal information and to let them know she oversaw the children just like the social worker suggested, in case of an emergency.

The next day Grace woke up two hours earlier than usual and then woke up her three boys and everyone else to shower and eat breakfast. She drove to six different schools.

She did that every morning and every afternoon. Then she would come home, wash everyone's clothes, clean the house, go grocery shopping, and cook for everyone. It was a lot of work, but she did everything with so much love.

Lucia called her one day and asked if she needed help, but she also said, "If you do, I would have to cancel appointments." Grace responded, "No, I don't want you to do that." Since Lucia had a huge family, she knew the importance of her working.

One of the hardest things for Grace was dropping off her friend Susana's younger son, who was only five years old. He would ask her every day before getting dropped off at day care, "When am I going to see my mommy? I want to go home, and I want to see my dog." Then he began to cry.

This was heartbreaking. Grace would always find the right words to encourage him. He was such a good, caring, and sweet little boy. Grace knew he was suffering.

Every day was very challenging for Grace, but she loved these children.

Thank God for Susana's oldest daughter. She took the role as a mom. She was caring and gentle with her younger siblings. She would try everything to help her little brother feel better. In the morning, Grace would drop him off at day care and the teachers would tell her how he was having a very hard time. Grace wouldn't explain too much to the teachers except to be patient with him since his family was going through a very hard time. She also told them she was his foster mom for now.

One day Grace received a call from the social worker, who gave her great news: the children's parents were out of jail. Grace was so happy! The only thing the social worker said was they couldn't move in with their parents yet. She also explained to Grace the children were going to have supervised visits with their parents once a week and Grace needed to drop them off at her office and pick them up afterward.

Grace picked up the children from school and gave them the good news about their parents being out of jail and how they were going to see them on supervised visits. The children were so happy. Susana's oldest daughter told Grace, "Sometimes we feel like we are the only ones going through something like this."

Grace explained how there were many other families struggling with different problems, not only them.

They all went out to eat that day to celebrate the great news. They had a lot of fun. They enjoyed their meal. It was one happy day.

It was a Friday afternoon when Grace took the children on their first visit with their parents. They arrived at the social worker's office. Unfortunately, only their mom showed up, but the children were so happy. Grace waited outside.

After the visit was over, it was hard for the children and Grace because their mom was crying and the children were crying, especially the little one. Grace started wondering if this was a good idea after all. Because of the suffering, they would take the youngest son, crying all the way, home. It was so emotional for everyone.

One day after picking everyone from school, Grace got a phone call from a new social worker who asked many questions to get caught up with the case. One of the questions was "Where do these children sleep?"

Grace responded, "They all sleep together in one bedroom. There are two beds where girls sleep with girls in one and boys with boys in the other."

The social worker said, "You can't have boys and girls sleeping in one bedroom together."

Grace explained to her that they were brothers and sisters. The social worker responded, "It doesn't matter." She also said, "We need to find a new house for them, if you don't have more rooms available."

All Grace was thinking at the very moment was about the children. Since they had been through so much, what would this do to them? Grace quickly took everything out of her master bedroom. She thought, *If I can put all the boys there, I can take a small room and put the girls in one room since there are only three bedrooms in my house.*

Grace worked hard all day. Then she contacted the new social worker and told her what she had done with the rooms. Grace added, "My master bedroom will be for the five boys, one room will be for the two girls and the other one for my husband and me."

The social worker answered, "Look! I understand how much you want to help these children, but we cannot have more than five people in one room. It is not safe." She added, "This happens to many children. They are not the only ones. We have more children than we have houses."

Grace knew in her heart there was nothing else she could do except pray for these children.

The next day, the social worker called Grace and told her, "We found two families who will take the children." She also told Grace that they were going to separate the children—the two youngest and the two oldest.

Grace told the social worker how hard it had been for the youngest. The social worker responded, "I understand, but we must do this. No one will take four children."

Grace then contacted the children's mom and told her what was going to happen with her children. She also asked her, "Is there anyone in your family that can take them?"

Susana explained, "They are trying, but we must wait."

Grace sat in her living room with all her family, including her foster children, and said to them, "I tried everything, but they have decided to move you to another house. She explained the reason why. "Not only that, but you will also be separated." This was so hard to say, but Grace knew it was the right thing to do. She had to be honest. Seeing the children's faces was so hard.

She also said, "The good news is it won't be for long. I spoke to your mom today, and she said some of your family members are trying everything possible to see if you can all go live together with one of them."

The children were sad and very discouraged.

The day arrived. Grace couldn't sleep all night. She woke up and made breakfast, and no one was talking. It was a quiet morning. Grace couldn't say much; she knew she had to be strong for the children and didn't want to cry in front of them.

Grace helped the children to get all their belongings together. The doorbell rang, and Grace's heart began pounding. She thought that if she felt nervous, she wouldn't want to imagine how the children must be feeling, and there was nothing she could do anymore.

The social worker began putting all their stuff in the back of a van, while Grace hugged all the children and kept reassuring them that everything was going to be OK. The social worker took the youngest child, put him in a car seat, got in the car, and began to drive away. Grace's tears started coming down her cheeks. She could finally let out everything she had been holding inside her for a long time.

Time passed, but one afternoon, Grace got a call from the children's mother, who said that some family members qualified to take all four children to their house. This was one of the happiest moments for Grace and all who loved these children. Susana told her all four children were going to her husband's sister's house.

This time, Grace was crying of happiness. She told her family everything that had happened, and they prayed to thank God for helping these children get reunited with their family.

Susana and her husband continued getting help. Susana bought a new car and found a great job doing what she loved. People from her church helped her clean her house, and she couldn't wait to have her children back with her. She finished all her classes, did everything the judge said, and everything was going great.

The day finally came. Susana went to court, took all the evidence of everything she had accomplished, and finally the judge said she could have her children back. They were reunited with their parents.
This was one of the happiest days for everyone, especially the children. It was a day no one would ever forget after so much struggle, sadness, and difficulties. Everyone was so happy and very grateful that the nightmare was completely over. They were finally together again back in their house.

Grace learned a huge lesson. She realized that parents' wrong decisions or right decisions have a huge impact on children's lives. She was never going to forget the whole experience. She was grateful she got to learn what parents, teachers, families, friends, and especially children must go through when poor or bad decisions are made. She also learned that everybody deserves a second chance and everyone can turn their life around, become even better than before, and start over the right way.

Grace continues helping people to this day. She knows she can't help everyone out there, but with one person she helps, she can change an entire generation.

Grace has some advice for you today. To all children in foster homes, God is watching over you. He loves you more than you can ever imagine. To the parents, you can always start over and do things right this time. To the teachers, thank you for your hard work with foster children and all children having difficulties. To the families, never stop trying to help each other.

And everyone reading this, share this story with someone who needs it.

Finally, live every day with a grateful heart, and treat everyone kindly. You don't know what someone is facing at this very moment. Maybe you are the answer they've been praying for.

Printed in the United States
by Baker & Taylor Publisher Services